Ling and the Turtle

Alison Hawes
Illustrated by Franco Rivolli

A turtle was on the soft sand.

"Help me!" she said.
"I am sinking!"

Ling lifted her out.

“Thank you,” said the turtle.

The next day,
Ling was out in his junk.

“Help me!” he said.
“I am sinking!”

The turtle saw Ling.

She lifted him out of the sea.

She took Ling back to the junk.

"Thank you," said Ling.
"Thank you," said the turtle.